"For I know the plans I have for you," declares the
you and not to harm you, plans to give you]
Jeremiah 29:11 (NIV)

Amazing Grace, Amazing Gifts

Autism and the gifts God granted along our journey

Written by

William Andrew Rose &
Terri Cunningham Rose

Copyright © 2021 Terri Cunningham Rose and William Andrew Rose.

All rights reserved. No part of this book may be used or reproduced by any means, graphic, electronic, or mechanical, including photocopying, recording, taping or by any information storage retrieval system without the written permission of the author except in the case of brief quotations embodied in critical articles and reviews.

WestBow Press books may be ordered through booksellers or by contacting:

WestBow Press
A Division of Thomas Nelson & Zondervan
1663 Liberty Drive
Bloomington, IN 47403
www.westbowpress.com
844-714-3454

Because of the dynamic nature of the Internet, any web addresses or links contained in this book may have changed since publication and may no longer be valid. The views expressed in this work are solely those of the author and do not necessarily reflect the views of the publisher, and the publisher hereby disclaims any responsibility for them.

Any people depicted in stock imagery provided by Getty Images are models, and such images are being used for illustrative purposes only. Certain stock imagery © Getty Images.

Scripture quotations marked (NIV) are taken from the Holy Bible, New International Version®, NIV®. Copyright © 1973, 1978, 1984, 2011 by Biblica, Inc.® Used by permission of Zondervan. All rights reserved worldwide. www.zondervan.com The "NIV" and "New International Version" are trademarks registered in the United States Patent and Trademark Office by Biblica, Inc.®

Scripture marked (KJV) taken from the King James Version of the Bible.

ISBN: 978-1-6642-2626-5 (sc)
ISBN: 978-1-6642-2628-9 (hc)
ISBN: 978-1-6642-2627-2 (e)

Library of Congress Control Number: 2021904344

Print information available on the last page.

WestBow Press rev. date: 04/14/2021

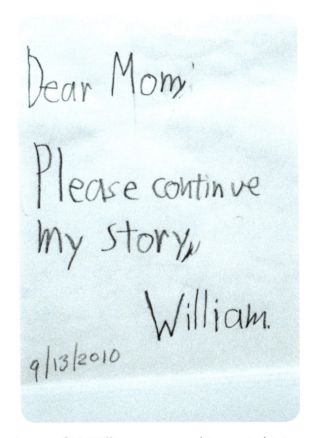

At the age of 10 William wrote me this note in his journal.
"Dear Mom Please continue my story"

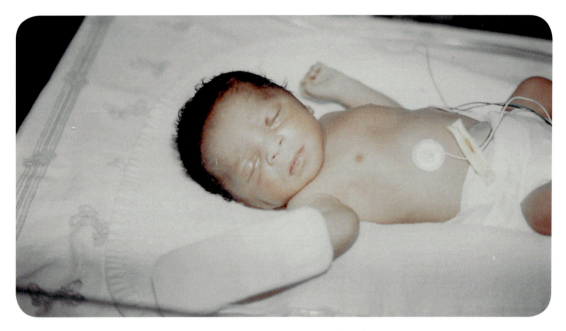

William in the hospital soon after delivery.

From birth I have relied on you; you brought me forth from my mother's womb. I will ever praise you.
Psalm 71:6 NIV

William's infant photo the day we took him home from the hospital.

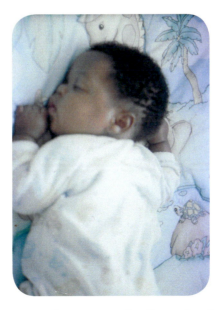

William napping at home a couple of months after his birth.

A Christmas trip to Nassau, Grand Bahamas in December of 1994 to visit friends and family.

Gratitude

To Bishop Harold Ray and Pastor Brenda Ray, thank you for your prayers, guidance, and support during the many hours of labor prior to the birth of William Andrew Rose. I will forever be grateful for your request for the doctors to deliver my son by emergency cesarean birth. William Andrew Rose (initials W.A.R. fits him perfectly) put up a good fight to enter this world, and he continues to do so today as he meets many challenges on a daily basis due to his disability. His faith in an unfailing God has allowed him to live a life of hope, joy, and perseverance.

Thank you to an amazing angel, Faith Clough, for your trust in a loving God that kept you praying for many days, hours, minutes, and seconds. You are a phenomenal woman of God, and on that day, 26 years ago, you played your role well as a true godmother.

Dedication

This book is dedicated to my three siblings, Meridith, Viola and my brother J.R.
Three of the best siblings anyone could ever hope for. You have loved and supported me over the years. Thank you for continuing to be there for me, and the seeds you have sown into my life.
I love you!!
-William

Gratitude

Cathy Feld, thank you for the love, care and concern that you had for my son as his Speech and Language Pathologist when he was just two years old. You gave me hope during the most challenging time of my life. You told me each time you met with my son what a great job I was doing as a Mom and, if it were not for me, William would not have been progressing the way he was. I will always be grateful to God for those words He allowed you to speak that gave me the encouragement I needed and the tenacity to fight for my son's rights over the years when I was faced with many challenges. I will forever be grateful for our friendship and the bond that God allowed to be created during this journey as a mother of a son diagnosed with Autism Spectrum Disorder. You are indeed "My Friend".

Ms. Cathy you were one of the first Speech and Language Pathologist to prepare me to tackle one of the most important barriers I wanted to overcome, communication. You have been kind and supportive to me and my mom throughout the years. You introduced us to your family, Matthew Feld and Aaron Feld, you witnessed my growth in wisdom, strength, compassion, trust, responsibility, and leadership. I am still not perfect in areas that I have yet to perfect, but I've accomplished what I have because of you, and for that I want to say thank you.

Cathy Feld, and I after my graduation from Jupiter High School

Gratitude

To Aaron Feld, thank you for the day 23 years ago when you took time from your busy schedule to sit at the piano with William and play for him. You were sowing a seed into his life for the love of music. He closed his eyes as you began to play a song just for him and was mesmerized by what he heard. That tiny seed was the door that God used to open up the mind of a little boy who was lost in his own little world. For that, I will always be grateful. You are family.

Mom, Aaron Feld and I at my high school graduation party. Brio Italian Grille, Palm Beach Gardens, FL. My favorite restaurant at the Palm Beach Gardens Mall.

Contents

Dedication viii
Foreword xiii
Preface xv
Chapter 1   "An Amazing Gift from God" 1
Chapter 2   "Becoming Socially Me" 7
Chapter 3   "My Love for Learning" 13
Chapter 4   "Challenges and Blessings" 24
Chapter 5   "In Pursuit of an Amazing Future" 32
Epilogue 46
Resources 61
Photo and Illustration Credits 64
Acknowledgements 65
Endorsement 66
About the Author, William Andrew Rose 68
About the Author, Terri Cunningham Rose 69

Mom what's wrong me?
William you have autism.

Foreword

There are not adequate words to express the deep love and respect that I have for my brother, William Andrew Rose. From the day that he was born his initials, W.A.R., proved that he would be a fighter who would rise above each of the challenges that he would face throughout his young life. I remember the day when William confidently proclaimed, "I will beat the odds of Autism." Indeed, he has overcome many obstacles that attempted to stand in his way. Little did we know at the time of his birth that terms such as speech delay, language delay, Pervasive Developmental Disorder-Not Otherwise Specified (PDD-NOS), and Autism Spectrum Disorder (ASD) would become frequently used in our family's vocabulary, and that I would become well versed in speech and language development and disorders.

William has amazed our family throughout the years with his many talents! The piano was the introduction to his love of music. William would often close his eyes and intently listen when a piano was being played, almost as if to become one with the music. Music "struck a chord" and resonated with him in a way that seemed to open a door that had previously not been unlocked. Throughout his childhood we readily recognized and encouraged the development of his innate musical abilities and other artistic gifts, which overtime became a part of his many expressive outlets.

As a child, I always wanted to become a pediatrician, and that dream stayed with me as I matriculated throughout my primary and secondary education. So much so, that I started my freshman year of college at the University of Florida as a Microbiology major with plans to attend medical school. However, once William was formally diagnosed with autism and started to receive in-home speech-language therapy services, I was determined to learn more about his diagnosis. My attempts to understand this unfamiliar developmental disorder that affects communication and behavior, led to me changing my major to Communication Sciences and Disorders. This was by far one of the best decisions that I have made in my life. Doing so allowed me to become a strong advocate for my brother during his education, from elementary school through college. Over the years, I participated in countless parent conferences, Individual Education Plan (IEP) meetings and other academic meetings, often assisting my mother in educating his teachers, school administrators, professors and university staff on his areas of strength and need. We discussed helpful strategies and accommodations, as well as the impact of his executive functioning weaknesses on his learning and academic performance. All of this was done in an effort to ensure that his educational needs were met and that his "voice" was heard.

Throughout the years, William has continued to impact the trajectory of my professional career. He is the reason that I obtained my bachelor's degree in Communication Sciences and Disorders from the University of Florida, a master's degree in Speech-Language Pathology and Audiology from Florida Atlantic University, a graduate certification in Applied Behavior Analysis from the Florida Institute of Technology, and continue to advocate for the clients and families who I have the honor and privilege to serve. My passion and dedication to them is most certainly due to him. I never would have imagined that my life's purpose would have been shaped so much by "my little brother" who now towers over me in height, but I am so thankful that it has been!

William and other individuals like him who are neurodiverse are such AMAZING GIFTS to this world! He has taught me valuable life lessons and has brought so much joy into not only my life, but the lives of many others. He is a kind, generous gentleman with a beautiful spirit and a heart of gold, who never ceases to amaze me! I am immensely proud to be his oldest sister and am tremendously blessed that he is my youngest brother. My prayer is that the GRACE that he extends to others in this ever-changing world, will be reciprocated and extended back to him.

Meridith Rose, MS, CCC-SLP
Speech-Language Pathologist
Owner of HomeTele SLP
www.HomeTeleSLP.com

Preface

I wanted to share my story because I have been dealing with the symptoms of my disability, autism, since I was diagnosed at the age of two. The strongest challenge I faced was being developmentally delayed. This affected my growth. I was sensitive about engaging with people that disliked, felt uncomfortable with or seemed to be uninterested in talking to me. Alongside that, stuttering kept me from speaking properly. As I grew, I encountered other kids who I wished I could have been able to communicate with. I wished I would have had the ability to learn their language. During those years in elementary school, I had many friends from the Hispanic community. Learning how to speak Spanish would have given me an opportunity to learn and understand their culture better, but that was not possible. The disability had delayed my speech, and I was limited in ways to communicate with them.

This whole experience throughout my life had a huge impact on my learning abilities in many areas. I struggled, but I have overcome. I have completed my Associate of Science Degree and I am now comfortable with who I am. I have many friends who respect me and have the patience I need them to have when we are together and having conversation.

I am here to encourage you to step out of your comfort zone, learn to accept who you are and inspire others. You will see as you read my book my faith has helped me, and yours will help you as well.

Amazing Grace, Amazing Gifts

An Amazing Gift from God

"Each of you should use whatever gift you have received to serve others, as faithful stewards of God's grace in its various forms."

1 Peter 4:10 (NIV)

Chapter One
"An Amazing Gift from God"

Amazing gifts are granted to talented people who are being discovered every day, through social media platforms, televised talent shows, local churches, and local clubs.

The discovery of any youth's talent, in many cases, begins in the home. From artists, to musicians, singers and computer whizzes, many of these talents cannot be taught but instead are amazing gifts from God. Some individuals diagnosed with Autism Spectrum Disorder (ASD) are known to be gifted in one area or another. William Andrew Rose's amazing gifts range from illustrated artist, to sculptor, painter, graphic designer and having the ability to play music by ear, including the piano, violin and the alto saxophone.

During William's first five years of life he had many challenges, some of which have continued to be a part of his life today. As a mother who researched ASD after her child was diagnosed, I read that it was recommended all children be screened for autism. All concerned caregivers should seek the advice of their child's pediatrician about ASD screening. Now, let's talk about William and the amazing gifts that God gave to him throughout his life.

William began having seizures as an infant after five days of labor and spending approximately one week in the hospital. It became known to me, during Williams first check-up, that his pediatrician was never contacted by the hospital and informed of his birth. One day as I was sitting with his sister Meridith, she held him in her arms and his eyes began to roll to the back of his head. It was very disturbing as my daughter and I witnessed William's first seizure. I took him to the doctor immediately and was referred to a neurologist. This would be the first of many appointments related to William's journey. As William grew, I kept my eyes on him and committed myself to observing and recognizing anything out of the ordinary. He never played with the mobile over his bed and other toys placed around him. He'd only stare at those toys. I played with William, and so did his other two siblings, Viola and J.R., in an effort to engage him.

As William began to grow, he attempted to coo and say 'mamma'. Yes, mamma!! I was so happy and excited to hear that word. Well, what mom would not be delighted to hear her son call her by name? A good friend of mine, Barbara Watson Haymon, was William's babysitter when I returned to work. She cared for William as though he were her own. Soon after she began to care for him, Barbara informed me that William cried continuously, non-stop. There was nothing she could do to comfort him. These were signs to me that something may be wrong. I decided to stay home instead of working to care for him myself. Months later, after William began walking and running around the house joyfully, he would become quiet. He no longer used my favorite word, 'mamma', but instead he would come to me, look towards me and turn around to run away. He would line up his mini cars in a row but wouldn't play with them. I didn't understand what was wrong.

One day early in the morning after the older kids had left for school, the alarm went off as I heard the door open. No one responded to my question, "Who's there?" I called for my son to come to me as I searched for him, but he did not appear. I went to my front door, and it was ajar. I looked outside, but no one was there. Then, I heard a voice, it was my neighbor. "Terri, William is here." I walked over and there was my son, quietly sitting in the swing set in the backyard of the house next to my neighbor's home. The owners of that home had moved out a few months earlier. This was my first experience with autism elopement. Autism elopement is when someone wanders off or disappears without your knowledge. It was a horrible feeling. Having a son who is non-verbal and incapable of responding to a mother's call made me feel frantic. I was thankful that those neighbors who left the swing set took their full-size German Shepherd with them!

My neighbor knew from this day forward to look out for William if she heard my alarm go off. It meant William Rose was on the run for an amazing adventure away from home to a swing set. As I spoke to William while he sat quietly in the swing, there was no eye contact. He did not respond to my questions. "William are you okay?" "William did you hear me when I called out for you?" He did not respond, and he had not come running to me with full joy as a child normally would at that age. Instead he just sat there, staring afar, because he was non-verbal; he was autistic. This was the first of many days my son wandered away from home to this abandoned swing set. My only que that he had left our home would be our burglar alarm system sounding off with a beep. That beep informed me that someone was either entering or exiting our home while the alarm was set. I didn't understand how my son knew the swing set was there at the beginning of his first adventure, or why this became his place of refuge on a daily basis, but I did know two things--God had protected him, and the swing provided comfort and peace for him as he remained in his own little world.

I took William to the pediatrician, Dr. Lynda Bideau, and explained to her what had been taking place since our last visit. I told her that William seemed a little distant when I spoke to him. She informed me that boys were slow and sometimes it takes longer for them to catch up. I explained to her that it was different. I worked in the childcare field and there was something wrong. There was no eye contact and he was not attempting to communicate or have conversation. She asked me to give him some time. William soon started using one-word sentences and pointing to items if he wanted something. He had three siblings who were there at his beck and call. They loved their brother, and we worked as a team to make sure his needs were met.

One day I noticed when I asked William questions, he would only repeat my words and not give me an answer. During this time, he also began to try a few more words than usual, but all that would come from his mouth was babbling. He was trying very hard to communicate, and I could tell he was becoming frustrated. He often banged his head on the wall in the hallway. My heart was broken. My son was trying to communicate and was frustrated because he could not. I hugged and comforted him so he would understand that he was loved and my main priority. I also tried to encourage him by explaining to him that it was going to be okay. We returned to the pediatrician. I expressed to her what I was witnessing at home regarding William's behavior. She informed me that *echolalia* is repetitive speech by a child learning to speak.

There were other things that irritated William from day to day. Anytime I would move the furniture around in the living room to clean he would cry, pushing on the furniture trying to put it back in its place. He did not like changes. Everything in his life had to remain the same. I also expressed my concerns to the doctor about William covering his ears all the time. Dr. Bideau gave me a referral for William to see a speech and language pathologist. She ordered a hearing test there in her office, which came back within normal range. She explained that William had symptoms of delayed speech and she wanted him to begin speech therapy immediately. We chose Easter Seals of Palm Beach County.

By the age of three, William began to love music. He could not communicate verbally, but he could sing, and boy did he love singing. William found a way to express himself through music. He was now able to engage with other children by singing in our special events children's choir at our church, Christ Fellowship. To me, this was amazing, and it was music to my heart just to hear William sing. One day we were invited to a friend's home who was a speech and language pathologist. Cathy Feld adored William. William sat at her piano and listened as her son, Aaron Feld, played a song for him. As we sat and talked, I noticed that William was sitting very still and attentive. He was no longer moving around or trying to express himself as he normally did in the company of others. As I continued to watch William sitting on the piano stool next to my friend's son, I noticed his eyes were closed. As I paid closer attention, I realized he was listening to the piano. He was taking it all in. He looked as though he was mesmerized by what he was hearing, like the music was touching the depths of his little soul. He continued to sit there quietly, listening with his eyes closed, until Aaron completed the song he was playing for William on the baby grand piano. Once the music ceased, William opened his eyes. We were amazed as he continued to remain quiet for a few moments. William's speech was limited, so he said nothing after the piano stopped playing. He loved music more than I realized. The piano was different, this experience had done something special to my son on this particular day. From that day forward, I played multiple genres in my home.

I knew after that piano experience that William needed a piano of his own. I strongly felt that music was going to be the key to unlocking the world that my son was living in all alone. His cousin, Charles McCray, owned a piano moving company. Charles found a used piano for William at the price of $300.00. I purchased the piano and Charles delivered the piano to our home. William was thrilled that he now had his own piano. His sister Viola would spend time with him at the piano, both siblings learning to play together.

In preparation for William's first year of preschool, he attended a summer program at First Baptist Church of West Palm Beach, Florida with his cousin, Taylor Joseph. She adored William and treated him like a brother. He enjoyed his summer at First Baptist and was ready to attend year-round preschool. We chose Noah's Ark in Loxahatchee, Florida. The director, Susan Sims, was very loving, kind, supportive and very observant regarding the students who attended school there. William enjoyed going there and was always very happy when I dropped him off at school. His classroom teacher was very kind and patient with William as well. Mrs. Sims notified me one day and informed me that William was not meeting the typical developmental milestones for a child his age and could not follow simple instructions or directions. She stated that William was unable to stand in a line or wash his hands and dry them during restroom time. He would only stand in front of the bathroom sink and allow the water to run over both of his hands. During this particular time, William had begun to talk, but continued to be limited in speech and language. He used very few words and mostly one-word sentences.

My cousin Taylor Joseph and me.

I contacted Dr. Bideau and took William in for another evaluation. She asked me to take William to the neurologist he had seen previously as an infant when he first experienced seizures. Once we arrived, the neurologist and about five graduate students entered the exam room. During our visit the neurologist informed me that William had autism. I questioned him about his diagnosis, asking him if he was sure and the neurologist said, "That's all you're going to get. You see these gray hairs in my head? I know what I'm talking about." Those five graduate students stood there with stunned looks on their faces, and so did I. It was unprofessional for the neurologist to have spoken to me in the manner he had, especially in front of the students. I refused to accept what he was saying to me and left his office upset. I decided after some research and speaking to an autism specialist that the symptoms William was exhibiting were in line with a diagnosis of Autism Spectrum Disorder.

I took William to the library weekly and checked out books. I made sure he had a couple of educational videos as well. We went to the park in our community, where I laid a large comforter on the grass. Face to face on our bellies I read and spoke to William. I did not know the proper way of assisting an autistic child with regard to maintaining eye contact, but this was the way I, a desperate Mom, decided to do it. Each time we went to the park, this was our routine.

William was now three and a half years old. In February of 1998 I was diagnosed with stage 2 breast cancer. I battled cancer and endured six months of chemotherapy. During this time William was not communicating well and was diagnosed with a speech and language delay. I wondered if he would ever be able to communicate effectively. My faith in an unfailing God gave me the tenacity to fight for my life, and the strength to persevere as I continued to seek the services that my son so desperately needed.

Becoming Socially Me

"Make a joyful noise unto the Lord, all ye lands. Serve the Lord with gladness: come before his presence with singing. Know ye that the Lord he is God: it is he that hath made us, and not we ourselves; we are his people, and the sheep of his pasture. Enter into his gates with thanksgiving, and into his courts with praise be thankful unto him and bless his name. For the Lord is good; his mercy is everlasting; and his truth endureth to all generations."

Psalm 100:1-5 (KJV)

Chapter Two
"Becoming Socially Me"

The Montessori Method was recommended to me for a child diagnosed with Autism Spectrum Disorder by a specialist. There was a Montessori preschool near our home in Palm Beach Gardens, Florida. I enrolled William there, and he loved the school and playing with his friends. One classmate was very caring for her young age. When I arrived to pick William up, she would be playing with him in the classroom. There was another little preschooler who was quiet and shy like William. I think that is what drew them to each other. They would be playing on the playground on days when I picked him up from preschool. During his months at the Montessori school, I found out that William was gifted in art. One day as I arrived to pick William up from school, the teacher provided me with a picture he had drawn. The teacher stated that William was very good at drawing, compared to other classmates his age. I looked at the picture and was very surprised by the details in the drawing. On other days when I arrived to pick William up, I would find him in a special place where he loved to play with the other kids. He described it to me as a 'giant tall bunk bed'. When I saw it for the first time, I looked down at William, smiled and said, "That's a loft William." This loft that was built in the play area of the school, was the hang out spot for the kids.

William's fourth birthday was just around the corner. His party was scheduled to be at a new venue not far from the school. The kids loved the Playmobil Fun Park, and all of his classmates were invited. He had a wonderful time dancing with one of his favorite classmates who spent time with him at school. Since William did not like the typical cake, he asked me if he could have an ice cream cake instead from Carvel. Vanilla ice cream with chocolate crumbles was his favorite. William enjoyed his ice cream cake and had an amazing fourth birthday party. William was talking more and was learning to socialize with other children his age.

Dancing with one of my friends at Playmobil Fun park during my fourth birthday party.

Enjoying my birthday party.

William later attended a pre-school where my girlfriend Michelle Hildreth's son, Sean, had been attending. The Nativity School, which was also located in Palm Beach Gardens, was his new preschool. William adjusted well since Sean was there, and he loved his teacher. He took naps and enjoyed making new friends. He participated in a small program at the end of the school year. William's teacher and the director of the school were great. They were kind, patient and understanding.

At home, William loved our desk top computer. I was very surprised to see how well he caught on, and how much he was interested in learning how to use the computer. William loved a collection of children's computer games called the Little Critters. "Mommy and Me" was one of his favorites. He played the interactive games over, and over again. He also loved the Magic School Bus. I learned early on that William loved science. He was always asking me to purchase science project kits, which he enjoyed.

One particular Christmas, William loved rewinding the VCR repeatedly. The movie William came to enjoy during the holidays was Miracle on 34th Street, an old Christmas classic. He giggled as he enjoyed Kris Kringle's character revealing to a little boy that he was actually Santa Claus. As men in the scene laughed at the boy's belief in Santa, Kris Kringle bends down to the little boy's ear and whispers, "I am." The startled look on the little boy's face made William's day. He replayed that scene over and over again and laughed until he became tired. William sat in front of the television throughout the week rewinding the video tape repeatedly to see the little boy startled by Kris Kringle's response.

William continued receiving speech services at Easter Seals of Palm Beach County, and later at St. Mary's Hospital. St. Mary's speech department had a wonderful speech and language pathologist who worked well with William by the name of Patrick. It was at St. Mary's that William was evaluated and diagnosed with hyperlexia (precocious reading ability in very young children).

William: I loved the rolling displays in the library and the computers that had the installed software/cd rom games. These were educational games which we did not have at home. I was able to play games like The Magic School Bus, which was a science educational game, the Disney Interactive programs, which were multiple educational games and Jump Start, which was a series of math games. The library was a wonderful place to visit because it opened up my mind to learning, new adventures and education.

William also enjoyed reading every sign he saw as we drove throughout the community. He would also remember the words from books I'd read to him before and would pretend he was reading to me word for word. I made sure to locate resources that would assist William with articulating his language, and for programs to enhance his socialization skills. William also began enjoying various types of outdoor sports.

Our place of worship, Christ Fellowship in Palm Beach Gardens, Florida, has a horseback riding ministry for special needs kids. Once I signed William up, he enjoyed going to horseback riding classes, but he did not like touching horses because of sensory challenges related to Autism Spectrum Disorder. William was placed on the saddle for the first time and with the help of two wonderful assistants he learned to focus, held on to the reins and positioned his feet where they were supposed to be in the stirrups. William started talking more during those sessions than he ever had before. It made me very happy that his speech and language were beginning to improve more than ever. The individuals that were there to assist William made sure he had the perfect posture, and they assured him that he would not fall off the horse. They worked with him very well and cared for him during each session to make sure he was feeling confident as he learned how to ride.

Thank you, Christ Fellowship Pastors, Tom and Donna Mullins and Pastors, Todd and Julie Mullins, for going above and beyond for special needs children who attend your church and who are a part of our community. We love you all and appreciate everything that you have done through this ministry for our families. Thank you for giving William and I a place we can call "Home".

William:

A wonderful Christian man who was a shadowing ministry volunteer at Christ Fellowship provided my mom with an opportunity to go to service in peace without having to worry about me. Mr. Randy was a very kind man and took good care of me. The Special Needs Ministry Horseback Riding Program at Christ Fellowship stimulated my speech. My mom has always told me that this was the first time that I started using my expressive language skills. My first horseback riding took place in 2005. I did not like touching the horses because of the texture of the horse's hair, but I enjoyed riding. Go to gochristfellowship.com for more information regarding this God-given, special needs ministry.

Enjoying Sunday morning childcare at Christ Fellowship

Enjoying horseback riding at Christ Fellowship's special needs ministry horseback riding program.

I enjoyed playing soccer at Lake Worth Parks and Recreation Center.

A day at the stadium on the track field.

A day of tennis with my brother J.R.

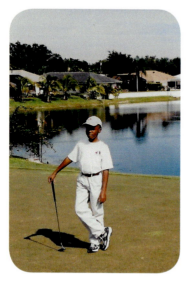

I enjoyed learning how to play golf at the USGA/PGA of America First Tee program.

A visit to Islands of Adventure

My Love for Learning

"The heart of the discerning acquires knowledge, for the ears of the wise seek it out."

Proverbs 18:15 (NIV)

Chapter Three
"My Love for Learning"

At the age of five years old, I enrolled William into Trinity Christian School of Palm Beach Gardens for kindergarten. Mrs. Mary Roos was an amazing kindergarten teacher. She worked diligently with William preparing him for first grade. She focused on phonics, reading and arithmetic until William was able to master them on his own. She did a wonderful job making sure he understood all of his academics. This wonderful teacher would provide extra work for me to work with William at home. She was very patient, loving and caring. She kept me informed of his progress and would share with me those special moments that William had throughout his day. William had many friends in his classroom and she always made sure he was included during any of the activities and the special events that she had planned for the children during after school hours. All of the parents of the students in the kindergarten class were very nice and invited William to parties and outside activities their children were involved in so William could socialize. William sometimes enjoyed spending time playing inside of the playhouse on the playground. It was a wonderful experience for William at Trinity Christian School as he struggled through challenges of language expression and other executive functioning skills. His teacher was a true angel that I know God gave to William to prepare him for entering primary school. Sadly, she passed away at the end of that school year. William and the students from her class attended the memorial service.

William:

Attending Trinity Christian School of Palm Beach Gardens was a blessing. My kindergarten teacher, Mrs. Mary Roos, provided the basic educational foundation that I needed to accomplish my goals. Without her, I would not have had the skills or confidence to succeed in elementary school, middle school, high school or college. I accomplished them all because of the love and care she provided during kindergarten. For that I will always be grateful, and she will always have a special place in my heart.

My kindergarten teacher Mrs. Mary Roos.

"Love is patient, love is kind. It does not envy, it does not boast, it is not proud. It does not dishonor others, it is not self-seeking, it is not easily angered, it keeps no record of wrongs. Love does not delight in evil but rejoices with the truth. It always protects, always trusts, always hopes, always perseveres. Love never fails."
1 Corinthians 13:4-8 (NIV)

My kindergarten graduation at Trinity Christian School of Palm Beach Gardens.

During the summer after kindergarten, I decided I would homeschool William for his first two years of elementary school. William could use these extra two years to receive additional speech therapy during the week, as well as, occupational therapy, to assist with his handwriting skills. William's speech and language therapy services continued. His new speech and language pathologist, Sofia Tzavaras, at the Rehabilitation Center for Children and Adults in Palm Beach, Florida was one of the best. We are grateful for her hard work and dedication in assisting William with reaching each of his goals.

I enjoyed home schooling William. Each year I was required to have a teacher evaluate him, and later I would complete a home school application for the following year. There was a very nice elementary school teacher, three doors down from our home. She was more than happy to evaluate William each year per the school district's requirements. William enjoyed his home school days. I used a portion of a curriculum shared by home schooling parents along with the Abeka curriculum. I loved the fact that Abeka was Christian based and it provided the Christian foundation that William continued to need in his day to day life. He enjoyed English, history and math. I attended home-school meetings for parents and exchanged curriculum ideas. Home school students are eligible for therapy services through the school district. William received speech services at Grove Park Elementary, which was our assigned school.

William loved science, so we created a vegetable garden in the back of our home. He learned to prepare the soil prior to planting seeds in our garden with his brother J.R. William and I spent time watching birds nesting in our orange tree in the back yard. We enjoyed watching the bees from the indoor window during the pollination period when they were attracted to the flowers. William loved the orange aroma and brought the blooms inside and placed them inside of a glass of water. After the oranges grew on the tree, he helped pick them during harvest time.

William and I also went on many field trips. A couple of those were the Maritime Museum, and the Martin Luther King Memorial on Flagler Drive in West Palm Beach, Florida. Throughout the summer William continued to draw and enjoy music.

I enjoyed being home schooled by my Mom. It provided that special time for the two of us to bond and spend time together.

During home school hours I enjoyed science and learning about gardening and the process of pollination. Here I am picking orange blossoms from our orange tree.

I grew my own tomato garden.

I enjoyed spending time working on my computer playing educational games.

The Maritime Museum was one of my favorite places I enjoyed visiting.

My Friends and I at Palm Beach Public Elementary School after our fifth grade graduation ceremony.

After a particular day of home schooling, I was in the kitchen cooking dinner and heard someone playing the piano. It was the tune to the song "Amazing Grace". I didn't say anything, I just listened. The song would play a little, the pianist would miss a note, and then start all over again. This repeated until the song was played all the way through without any errors. When the song had been played for the last time beautifully, I clapped my hands and gave the ovation that was so well deserved. "Good job, Viola!" I said to whom I thought was the mystery piano player. To my surprise a tiny voice said with excitement, "This not Viola, this William!" My, I was shocked! I almost fainted. This seven-year-old had taught himself how to play "Amazing Grace" on the piano without any piano lessons. I had never heard the song on the radio in my home before, or at the church we attended. The only thing I could think of was that he may have heard it during a commercial advertisement that played hymns on the television. Later that week, I signed William up for piano lessons. William became interested in classical and popular music. He enjoyed listening to Bach, Beethoven, Mozart and Gershwin to name a few. He enjoyed going to his piano lessons, but always complained about how it hurt his hands when he played. The teacher recommended using a tennis ball, but it didn't help. He did not embrace it in a way that I had hoped, but he continued to love music and would play the piano with his sister Viola.

At the age of seven, the pediatrician, recommended we see a new pediatric neurologist. It was also time for William to take a shot at elementary school. With additional speech therapy and social skills groups, I felt he was ready. He was doing great and I was proud.

My wonderful friend Michelle's two children Sean and McKenzie Martin attended Palm Beach Public Elementary School String Program. I looked into it for William. As summer approached, I realized William needed to be introduced to the violin since I was considering enrolling him at Palm Beach Public. I contacted Lynn University in Boca Raton, Florida, and found out that they had a violin program on Saturdays that I could enroll William in. Unfortunately, he did not have a violin. At a Tai Chi class one weekend, I met a very nice young lady. As we talked about our children, I told her William needed a violin so he could learn to play. She said to me, "I have a violin that he can use." I was shocked. What are the chances that this could happen? But for the amazing grace of God! He is our provider. She met with me at my home and gave the violin to William. We started violin classes at Lynn University immediately, and William went every weekend for lessons. William did extremely well and learned very quickly to play the violin (surprisingly, by ear), without using the music book. I realized in that moment William had been gifted by God to play multiple types of instruments.

William was accepted into the strings program for the following school year at Palm Beach Public Elementary School. William's two close friends, Sean and McKenzie, had enjoyed the strings program so William was confident he would enjoy it as well. Mr. Andrew Matzkow, Music Director/Choice Program Coordinator of the Palm Beach Public Strings Program, welcomed William and supported him throughout his years at Palm Beach Public Elementary School. William's third grade teacher, Carrie Reynnells, was very patient and worked well with William. She attended his Individual Education Plan (IEP) meetings and expressed William's needs. She advocated for my son, even though it was challenging during those meetings to request the services she felt would be beneficial for him. The effort she put forth made me very satisfied that she was his teacher. William was inspired by many teacher's at Palm Beach Public, his fourth-grade teacher, Ms. Hernandez; his fifth-grade teacher, Ms. Gray; his physical education teacher, Ms. Dana Rapport; and a school resource teacher who pulled William from his class to assist him with reading and language arts, Mrs. Wendy Bieneman.

During the years he attended Palm Beach Public Elementary School, William received speech therapy under the guidance of Speech and Language Pathologist, Ms. Debbie Tuliano. William was also pulled out of class for special services because of his diagnosis.

William continued to enjoy art at this age and loved his art teacher, Ms. Davis. She spent extra time with William in her classroom, assisting him as he continued to embrace art in a way I would have never imagined. William also attended The Robert and Mary Montgomery Armory Art Center on the weekends and during the summer months. He would attend each summer until early high school. Many of William's art pieces were entered into various art exhibits at the Armory Art Center. The instructors started informing me about how talented William was in clay modeling, painting and of course, illustrated art.

William was blessed to be talented in so many areas, and it made me even more proud as his talents evolved. I spoke to one of our Palm Beach County Commissioners, Addie L. Green, about how wonderful the strings program was at Palm Beach Public Elementary School, and what this program had done for William. Commissioner Green was invited to come and listen to the students play during one of their school performances. She attended and enjoyed the performance. William enjoyed playing his violin in the Palm Beach Public Elementary School Orchestra.

William:

At the age of nine, I started attending Palm Beach Public Elementary School. I enjoyed playing my violin in the orchestra. I was nervous because of my inner struggles with my Autism diagnosis. I was dealing with new students who were welcoming me. Although I felt intimidated by one teacher, over time I was able to embrace the cooperation and support provided by the principal, vice principal, teachers and staff. I had to receive help from my therapist in order to overcome my experience. Throughout my time at the school, I learned more about art and how to play my instrument, which were essential to my journey later on in my life. At the same time, my teachers wanted me to focus on my assignments and tests so I could do well in my academics.

My experience at the Armory Art Center was phenomenal. The different genres of art were all new to me. I enjoyed my time working outside in the fresh air. I was able to focus more because being outside opened the space where I worked. Sculpting clay piqued my interest in providing a new prospect of making art more physical. And of course, my most creative area of art is traditional illustration. Using a pencil to sketch the best ideas in a simple form allows me to outline my draft and reevaluate my key points of the drawing.

Ms. Carrie Reynnells, my third-grade teacher, Mr. Andrew Matzkow, Music Director/ Choice Program Coordinator of the Palm Beach Public Strings Program, and I.

Mom and I after one of my performances at
Palm Beach Public Elementary School.

Then Commissioner Addie L. Green
and I at Palm Beach Public.

Challenges and Blessings

"The Lord is my rock, my fortress and my deliverer; my God is my rock, in whom I take refuge. He is my shield and the horn of my salvation, my stronghold."

Psalm 18:2 (NIV)

Chapter Four
"Challenges and Blessings"

In September of 2004, the children and I lost our home during Hurricane Frances. The kids and I left for Marietta, Georgia to stay with a relative, Hyram Mency, prior to the hurricane hitting Florida. Hyram, a loving cousin, took care of us until we were able to return home. William, did great, he thought we were on vacation and enjoyed every moment away from home. When we returned home, we were devastated to find all of our belongings destroyed. A portion of the roof had been torn off and the ceiling had collapsed. Mold was on everything. All of the hotels were full, and the insurance company was not responding fast enough. We ended up staying in that home for a few days until the insurance company paid for the living expenses. Now a second hurricane was coming. We found a place to rent on the same day Hurricane Jeanne was to arrive in Florida. We would receive a direct hit again in Palm Beach County. More damaged, our home was a complete loss and had to be demolished and rebuilt. It would take three years until we were able to rebuild from the ground up and return home. The Associated Press contacted me to do a story on our loss from the hurricanes. William was so excited when he saw the story online with our photo.

As a mother I was glad that we were all safe. On the other hand, William was extremely concerned about one thing; he wanted all of his old toys that were now gone. I tried to offer comfort, telling him he would receive new toys. He didn't care for anything new and cried saying he wanted his old things. The piano, which he loved to play on, was damaged beyond repair. It fell apart when the movers tried to lift it and take it to storage until we were able to rebuild. I went to Chafin Music in nearby Lake Worth, Florida to look at a used piano for William. The owner, Mr. Chafin, was very kind. I told him we were there to look at a used piano for my son, and what had happened to our old one. He looked at my son and told him to look at two different pianos that he pointed out and asked my son to choose the one he wanted delivered to our home. I was speechless and immediately expressed my appreciation. His daughter, Cathy Chafin, whom I had gone to school with reminded me so much of her dad, and now I knew why. Her father had instilled something wonderful into his children—kindness. The piano arrived and William was very happy. This was a huge blessing for him. William's connection with music had returned to our home and he was at rest.

William tried out for Bak Middle School of the Arts Performing Arts Program. He had an interest to continue playing his violin for middle school. I will never forget the confidence William had prior to and after his audition. I asked him how he thought he had done. He said, "Great Mom, I did great" with enthusiasm. I was sure he would be accepted into the program, but sadly, he was not. He was very disappointed, but he quickly learned that sometimes things don't always work out the way we want them to. It also meant God had something better in store for him. It took a while to find the right school for William. I needed to make sure the school I chose would be suitable for his needs as he continued to struggle with language expression, processing information and other areas related to his executive functioning skills.

William was now getting excited about starting school again. I applied for the State of Florida's McKay Scholarship, and he qualified. The McKay Scholarship Program for Students with Disabilities provides the opportunity for an eligible student with a disability to attend a participating private school, and the program also offers parents public school choice. The eligible student can be transferred from a public school.

We applied to several of the private schools that accepted the McKay Scholarship. William was not accepted into two of those schools because of his challenges. For an entire school year, William transitioned to and from a number of schools because none of them could adequately address his educational needs. After diligently searching for an appropriate school setting, and with no results, I decided to work with William from home until the next school year began.

William and I used Dyer Park near our home for our physical education setting. William also participated in the PGA First Tee program, which is located on the same site inside of Dyer Park. This is where William learned to play golf. On one particular day there was a Christian school at the park with their students. I approached the gentleman in charge, and he was very pleasant. I told him about William, and our difficulty finding a school for him that would be able to meet his needs. He provided information about their school and asked me to stop by and speak with the front office. William and I visited the school the following day and were so excited because we had now found a school that could provide the services he was in need of. William started attending Lake Worth Christian School during the next school year for seventh grade.

During the first year at this school, I realized that William still had a love for math. It was his favorite subject when I home schooled him. His middle school math teacher, Mr. Bom, was very kind and patient with William. William had challenges with stuttering and could not understand why students did not have time to talk with him in the hallway. I explained to him that he needed more time because of his stuttering, they did not want to be late to class and the best time to talk to them would be during lunch time or after school. Two of his new school mates, Dana Goronsky and Kinsey Cresswell, were always there if he needed someone to talk to. He met them both on his first day of school. On his first day of school they were assigned to welcome and to assist him with adjusting to the campus. Dana Goronsky and Kinsey Cresswell continue to stay in touch with William on social media. Matt Abate, Jared Gaum, and Zach Russell were also great friends of William's. They were very patient and encouraged William to always do his best. These five students always made time to say hello and provided the patience needed to allow William to express himself during conversation. Another classmate, Dennis Glaser, was always there as a friend and on occasion spent time with William during afterschool hours.

William enjoyed singing in the choir and loved his music teacher, Mrs. Beth Acosta. She was very kind. William was interested in signing up for any program that would improve his social and language expression skills. Mrs. Acosta made sure William was included in drama camp for the summer, which was recommended by his new pediatrician, Dr. Ronald Romear. Dr. Romear was caring and very knowledgeable regarding Autism Spectrum Disorder. He made recommendations throughout William's academic years. In drama camp, William would become the narrator for some of the plays and enjoyed every moment of his involvement in the program, including assisting Mr. Rafael Acosta with setting up the stage props.

Mrs. Acosta was also the music director of the chorus and band at Lake Worth Christian School. William decided he wanted to learn how to play another instrument, the alto saxophone, which he mastered with the assistance and under the guidance of Mrs. Acosta. The saxophone was gifted to William by a very good family friend, Melanie Glinton-Grimes.

Mrs. Boswell taught William how to sew during drama activities. William received many awards for his participation in each of these particular performing arts areas.

Lisa Lennon is a professionally certified educational therapist trained by the National Institute for Learning Development (NILD.org). Through the Discovery program, Mrs. Lennon assisted William with any academic challenges while enrolled at Lake Worth Christian. A very kind and caring Christian woman who gave William all the time he needed to make sure he was successful academically, Mrs. Lennon helped William master everything she had taught him over the years through the Discovery program.

William:

I was a thirteen-year-old student who had recently enrolled at Lake Worth Christian School. I wanted to use my talents to assist me with communicating with my classmates. I was not able to communicate properly because of a stuttering condition. So, I decided to start drawing pictures of my friends at school, and it surprised me when they loved my illustrated artwork. Because of this, I was able to overcome my social issues, and my confidence level grew over time. My middle school art teacher, Ms. Joan Therien, assisted me with expressing myself through my artwork. Mr. Joe Baillargeon, Mr. Gary Welton, Mrs. Marie Giresi, Ms. Diane Allen and many other teachers provided guidance, mentorship, and support, which demonstrated the leadership I needed in a Christian environment.

Here I am sharing my illustrated drawing with my classmates from Lake Worth Christian School.

My friend Dennis Glacier, Shelby and Zach Russell and I at Lake Worth Christian School's annual carnival event

My classmate and best friend Dana Goronsky from LW Christian School who supported me over the years.

Some of the trophies and awards I received over the years.

William continued to enjoy going to the Palm Beach County Library. Anytime there was a special speaker that piqued William's interest, he wanted to go and hear them speak. Jan Kasoff was scheduled to be at the library on April 12, 2012. William knew Mr. Kasoff was an Emmy award winning technical director for NBC's Saturday Night Live, with 10 nominations and 6 wins during his career. I took William to hear him speak and when it was over William wanted to say hello. William was thrilled after he was allowed to see and hold one of Mr. Kasoff's actual Emmys and take a photo with him. That made William's evening, and it was something that William would never forget.

William's confidence grew more that year as he signed up to attend two conferences. One at the Able Trust Disability Conference in Tallahassee, Florida, and another in Orlando with our church, Christ Fellowship in 2013. Both of these opportunities allowed William to travel alone for the first time as he reached another milestone.

Jan Kasoff, Emmy award winning technical director for NBC's Saturday Night Live, and I at the Palm Beach County Library.

One day, William asked me to start a weekend program for students diagnosed with autism. He wanted students to be able to come together, socialize, make friends, learn life skills, job skills and have fun. I listened, and Aspies Connect was born. Life Span of Palm Beach County Executive Director, Teri Mitchell, provided the space for our program. Aspies Connect provided an opportunity for parents to have a three hour break away from their children as we supervised activities at local entertainment or educational venues. Parents were only required to pay for the cost of the activity. The William Sonoma store in the Palm Beach Gardens Mall provided free cooking classes, and Pottery Barn in City Place taught the students how to decorate their bedrooms and bathrooms. The Creatives at the Apple Store in the Palm Beach Gardens Mall taught students about technology and introduced them to the new iPad. It was a wonderful program, and the children and parents enjoyed it. Aspies Connect later evolved into an afterschool program, offering life, job and social skills. Olivia Giamanco was instrumental in helping to secure space provided by the Palm Health Care Foundation. She also assisted with marketing and other helpful resources.

Aspies Connect was a program that I felt was needed for parents and students like myself. All parents need a break, especially those who have children diagnosed with a disability. I enjoyed spending time with my new friends painting at a local venue, meeting at a local theater in Lake Park, bowling, playing games, and attending life skill programs. I was grateful for the volunteers who assisted and earned community service hours from Palm Beach Atlantic University, Taylor Schmidt, Anna Boatwright and Kelsey Taber, as well as students from The Benjamin School. We are in great need of these types of programs to enhance the skills needed for individuals on the autism spectrum.

My first Aspies Connect program held at Life Span of Palm Beach County.

An Aspies Connect program visit to the Apple Store in the Palm Beach Gardens Mall.

In Pursuit of an Amazing Future

"For I know the plans I have for you," declares the LORD, "plans to prosper you and not to harm you, plans to give you hope and a future."

Jeremiah 29:11 (NIV)

Chapter 5
"In Pursuit of an Amazing Future"

In January of 2013, William started attending Jupiter High School in Jupiter, Florida. William also received services that benefited him as he prepared to graduate. He was acquainted with students at church that attended Jupiter High and they made him feel at home. They became great friends and prayed together at the flagpole once a week in the morning before school.

During William's last few months of high school, I remember seeing his name on the school's board near the entrance as I arrived to pick him up one day. I was so surprised and proud to see the recognition regarding William's accomplishments and Grade Point Average (GPA). He worked extremely hard and graduated in May of 2014 with a 3.857 GPA from Jupiter High School. I was such a proud parent during the graduation ceremony. Now it was time to prepare him for college and the future he had with no limits.

William:

I loved spending time with my friends, Coach Dave Runner, and two of the other coaches, Mr. Kennerson and Mr. Molina. They helped students with disabilities understand social issues. The coaches would provide a social issue scenario and ask the students to find a way to resolve the social issue. I enjoyed it, because I was able to speak my thoughts properly, and it helped me with those scenarios if they happened in real life. I also appreciated my guidance counselor Ms. Janele Young. She was very supportive and made sure I had the services I needed as I completed my last two years of high school. My principal, Mr. Dan Frank, was also supportive, as many of the other staff at the school were. It was the perfect support team for me to complete the remaining years and become successful as I completed high school. I was involved in many activities. One of the activities was becoming a member of the National Honor Society. I tutored students at Jupiter Elementary School with other National Honor Society recipients. One of my favorite teachers at Jupiter High School was my Liberal Arts and Biology teacher, Mr. John Hetu. He took out a lot of time to help me to understand the projects and assignments, so I could further advance myself. He helped me to understand the importance of staying focused on the subject and its details. Mr. John Hetu, encouraged me to do my best.

Williams name and GPA posted on the board near the entrance of Jupiter High School.

My graduation photo from Jupiter High School

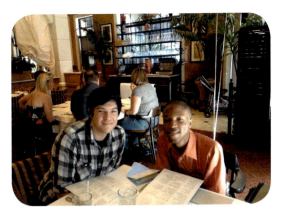

Matthew Abate, one of my best friends, celebrating my high school graduation with me at Brio Italian Grille, Palm Beach Gardens, FL.

College was always William's goal, and now the time had come. Alleluia!!!! William applied for financial aid and was considering two specific art schools: The Ringling College of Art and Design in Sarasota, Florida or Savannah College of Art and Design (SCAD) in Savannah, Georgia. At the last minute, William had a change of heart and decided that he did not want to attend school away from home. Instead, he decided on a university nearby to study psychology because of his Autism Spectrum Disorder diagnosis. William would turn 19 years old during the first week of college. A few of his friends who attended the university gathered and celebrated this milestone with him.

William packed and ready to go to live on campus at the university.

William and his friends celebrating his 19th birthday at the university.

During William's first semester, he met a major challenge. One particular psychology instructor stated they did not understand why students with disabilities bother to go to college. It was after this encounter William decided that he no longer wanted to study psychology. I was heartbroken. When I confronted the professor who made that statement, I was told of a student with a disability who had previously attended the university and was fired from their first job after graduation. That was the professor's reasoning for why disabled students should not attend college. God can do anything through these young individuals; they only need an opportunity.

William was subjected to multiple incidents of instructors not responding to his questions during class. Even though William was permitted by the university to record during class, he still needed the opportunity to ask questions. One incident was so overwhelming that William began to regress. After unsuccessful attempts to seek assistance from staff designated to accommodate students with disabilities and the school's administration, I scheduled an appointment for William to meet with his primary care provider. Once he was evaluated it was recommended that William drop out of that particular class. I received written documentation from the primary care provider and immediately delivered it to the administration. While walking on campus one day, William was approached from behind by the professor, (who was riding a bike) he questioned him about his absence from class, which frightened William and triggered his anxiety associated with Autism Spectrum Disorder. Unfortunately, the instructor had not been informed that William would no longer be attending his class. Communication among stake holders is of the utmost importance when dealing with students with disabilities.

Navigating higher education would prove difficult for William. A year and a half had now passed. I requested a meeting with the university's administration to discuss his special needs accommodations and solutions for his success. My daughter Meridith, who was inspired by William to pursue Speech and Language Pathology as a career, flew in to attend the meeting with us. I also invited a representative from the Center for Independent Living Options (CILO). Not only were our concerns not addressed William was chastised for recording class sessions even though his accommodations clearly permitted him to do so. It was at this time I was prompted to make a report to the Office for Civil Rights in Atlanta, Georgia. In the meantime, William set a goal to complete his general education courses at the university. Mrs. Andrea Macon, a retired English teacher, tutored William and assisted him with getting back on track to continue his studies.

During this time William lost his ability and drive to continue to draw as an illustrated artist, I was so upset. I took him to his neurologist who was unsure why William was feeling he had lost his ability to draw and felt he had to start over again to regain those skills. I purchased all types of art supplies to encourage him to try, but it did not work. Three months later on August 13, 2016, I returned home from work and William surprised me by sharing a beautiful picture that he had drawn. To God be the glory!!

"Consider it pure joy, my brothers and sisters, whenever you face trials of many kinds, because you know that the testing of your faith produces perseverance. Let perseverance finish its work so that you may be mature and complete, not lacking anything."

James 1:2-4 (NIV)

William's birthday was approaching, August 25th, and I decided to celebrate him after all he had gone through. I threw him a surprise party with friends he had known through the years. Some of his favorite friends such as Jefferson Mullins, Andre Woodside, Ethan Murray, Danny Ingram, Taylor Schmidt, Anna Wu Boatwright, Taylor Branham, Jana Espy, Maegan Bailus, Savannah Painter and many others attended.

My friend Jefferson Mullins and I during my 22nd birthday celebration at Season's 52 in Palm Beach Gardens, Florida.

Andre Woodside

Andre was a wonderful Christian young man, and an inspiration to me. He will be greatly missed by so many, because of his love for the gospel and our Lord and Savior Jesus Christ.

In the fall of 2016 William transferred to Palm Beach State College to study Graphic Design Technology. After facing many obstacles, we were able to reflect on his love for art. Palm Beach State College had a two-year program that was in line with the gifts God had instilled inside him. John Kiefer, head of the disability support department at the Palm Beach Gardens campus, and lead professor of the Graphic Design Department on the Lake Worth campus, Victoria Rose Martin, showed nothing but love, care and support during the years spent at Palm Beach State College.

Professor Jacques De Beaufort was William's Life Drawing professor and assisted William with improving accuracy and detail in his artwork. He challenged William to always take the time needed to create his best work possible. Professors Sherry and Wayne Stephens both instructed William at the Palm Beach State College Gardens Campus. They were very supportive during William's years there. William could count on Sherry being there for him anytime he called on her. Danielle Mitchell, and Heather Naylor were also very compassionate and caring professors at Palm Beach State College. God provided my son with angels for those years at Palm Beach State College, and I will always be grateful. William was inducted into Phi Theta Kappa Honor Society on December 5, 2017. His uncle, Steve O'Neal and close friends Andrew Magazine, and Chase and Chloe Camilli attended the induction ceremony. William also received special recognition at Palm Beach State College Academic Excellence and Leadership Awards ceremony and was chosen by John Kiefer to receive the Palm Beach State College 2018-2019 Above and Beyond Award for his efforts and strong work ethic. He graduated on the President's List with an Associate of Science Degree in Graphic Design Technology on May 8, 2019. William's diploma was presented to him by President Ava L. Parker of Palm Beach State College. He completed an internship in graphic design at our home church, Christ Fellowship in Palm Beach Gardens.

Proud to be honored to receive the Above and Beyond Award presented to me by John Kiefer Palm Beach State College Award Ceremony at the Wyndham Grand Hotel Jupiter, Florida

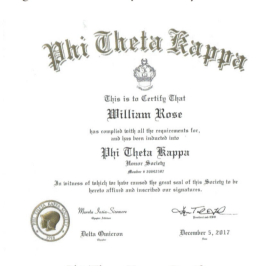

Phi Theta Kappa Certificate

Phi Theta Kappa members and I volunteering at the Big Heart Brigade

Uncle Stephen O'neal and I at my Phi Theta Kappa Induction Ceremony.

My friends Chloe and Chase Camilli at my Phi Theta Kappa Induction Ceremony.

William:

My final college years at Palm Beach State College were very important to me. Professor Victoria Martin has influenced me in so many ways, as well as many other professors on the Lake Worth campus. Their doors were always open when I needed assistance during my time there.

At the Palm Beach Gardens Campus Professor Wayne and Sherry Stevens, along with many other instructors, were extremely supportive. I am grateful to have had John Kiefer as my advisor to help guide me through each of my final three years. My grade point average soared during the first semester. I was offered an opportunity to become a member of the Phi Theta Kappa Honor Society, and I was inducted the same year. The honor society assisted me in becoming a better person as I improved my leadership skills.

My internship at Christ Fellowship's Studio B was a great experience. I learned a lot about graphic design in the workplace. I was grateful to have the privilege to collaborate with many professional graphic designers in Studio B. I will never forget the patience and kindness shown towards me during my internship. They had full respect and treated me as though I was a part of their staff.

Palm Beach State College President, Ava Parker, presenting me with my Associates of Science Degree Diploma.

My graduation cap I was proud to design for graduation day.

A memorable day, graduating from Palm Beach State College after five long years in college. It was worth it all.

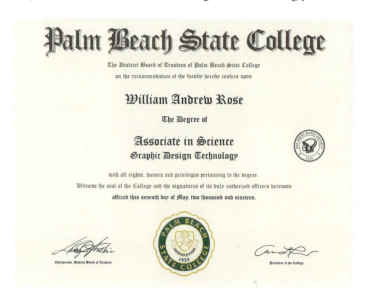

My Palm Beach State College Graduation Diploma

Since graduating from college, William continues to seek resources through organizations like Toast Masters International, and businesses like the Apple Store in the Palm Beach Gardens Mall. Toast Masters International is an educational club where William has learned public speaking and valuable leadership skills. As a Toast Masters member William continues to improve his expressive language skills. William also spends a lot of time at the Apple Store in the Palm Beach Gardens Mall. He enjoys assisting customers who attend the educational classes provided at no cost to participants.

Enjoying one of my Toast Masters International meetings.

William receives companion services through the State of Florida from the Agency for Persons with Disabilities (apdcares.org). Michael Demont, who is a provider for this agency, has been William's support coordinator and is one of the best in the industry. He along with Teylor Bean and Carolyn Moses have been a great asset to William. As companion care providers, both Teylor and Carolyn have worked on various projects with William.

Teylor has spent many hours with William at the Apple Store in the Palm Beach Gardens Mall taking a variety of "Today at Apple" sessions that he enjoys. Carolyn, a business teacher, has encouraged William's interest in starting a business by assisting him with Small Business Administration classes online. In addition, through the Center for Assistive Rehabilitation and Robotics Technology at the University of South Florida, Jeffrey Daniel has assisted William with accessing computer software and equipment.

William:

Toast Masters International has provided the confidence I need to become a better speaker. Mr. John Johnson and Mr. James Storms have been very supportive during my time as a member of Toast Masters International.

William:

The classes at the Apple Store are beneficial for me. The instructors are extremely patient when I attend the classes. I feel comfortable when I am in the Apple Store because the environment is very supportive. The staff allows me time to express myself during class. Now I have the knowledge and skills to assist others with Apple products, like my family and friends.

Assisting and educating people about their Apple products provides an opportunity for them to learn, and to adapt to new techniques and strategies to make their lives easier.

I have also enjoyed working with Teylor and Ms. Carolyn. They each have assisted me in areas that I have a great interest. Jeffrey Daniel and Michael Demont provided the support I needed during my last year of college. I appreciate each one of their visits to my home, and their encouraging words for me to continue to work hard in college, and life in general after college, regardless of all of the challenges that I may have to endure.

Jeff Daniels visit to our home to discuss my VR/DOE assistive technology needs for college. This agency provided my Apple Computer for my graphic design class.

Michael Demont and I after our monthly meeting regarding my Agency for Persons with Disabilities services.

Epilogue

Individuals diagnosed with Autism Spectrum Disorder have a right to be part of society just as anyone else. Individuals with disabilities have the right to receive accommodations and services that are allowed for anyone else to receive. As a parent of a child with a disability, I have had to learn how to fight. We must provide the support they need to become successful to the full extent of their potential. I will say it again: EVERYONE deserves an opportunity to be part of society, and no one has the right to refuse individuals with disabilities their legal rights. For more information please see the resource section at the end of the book.

God bless you on your journey,

Terri Cunningham Rose

William:

It's 2020. As I complete the vision to share my amazing journey, I have managed to set aside time for other interests. I enjoy singing and decided to join the Virtual Children's Chorus led by Sandi and Amisha Russell, directors of the Palm Beach Children's Chorus and the "Give Us Hope" project. To hear this amazing chorus, watch their YouTube video at: https://www.youtube.com/watch?v=pj9DvS57c30. You may also visit: www.virtualchildrenschorus.com and www.pbchildrenschorus.org.

Did I mention that I enjoy cooking? One of my favorite things is spending time in the kitchen. When I am cooking, the aroma from the herbs and spices calms my anxiety and allows me to enjoy that moment. The savory taste of food truly soothes the mind and soul. My favorite recipe I enjoy cooking often from one of my two cookbooks, Magnolia Table volume one and volume two, is chicken florentine. Joanna Gaines and Chip Gaines's (Magnolia Network) family recipes are the best. Simple and easy for "anyone" to follow! Thank you both for sharing these recipes, your cookbooks have made cooking so much easier for me.

Another one of my favorite things is spending time in the word of God. I have been studying and praying with my Christ Fellowship team weekly for many years. I have missed our in-person gatherings over the past months during the pandemic. For now, we are making it happen virtually until we meet again. I also enjoy my personal, signed daily devotional book, The Maxwell Daily Reader by John C. Maxwell. It's the best book to read to start my day. John C. Maxwell is one of my favorite speakers. I enjoy his messages when he visits our church.

Mrs. Bettye Knighton, a local publisher, has been assisting me with the start of my second book. She is a wonderful Christian woman. This is an illustrated book in full color about my life to encourage middle school, high school and college students who have been diagnosed with Autism Spectrum Disorder. The cover page of my second book is almost complete. Once it is done, I will begin to design the other pages, and with my Mom and Mrs. Knighton's assistance I will start working on the content.

I have also thought about sharing my story through film. One evening Mom and I were having dinner at Brio's in the Palm Beach Gardens Mall and Spike Lee entered the restaurant. I was star struck! I told my mom, who was in disbelief until I pointed out where he was seated in the restaurant along with his wife and others. I wanted to say hello, but my Mom told me it would not be appropriate to interrupt them. It would be great someday to meet Mr. Lee and talk about my story.

I was invited to apply for future openings at Apple, Inc. in December of 2019, prior to graduating from college. As an Apple employee I would be kept up to date on the development of new technology in the illustrated art industry and be at the forefront when new products are released. On April 1, 2020, I received an email from Apple Worldwide Recruiting. They informed me of a phone interview that will take place once their stores reopen. Our nation is currently dealing with a pandemic, similar to the Spanish Flu epidemic in 1918. Several businesses are currently closed, we are required to wear face masks in most public places and many church services are held online to avoid spreading the virus. Regardless of our current situation, I am hopeful because of my faith in God, and I am extremely excited about this potential opportunity because it will allow me to expand my creativity as an illustrated artist.

My long-term goal is to become self-employed as an illustrated artist. In other areas of my business as an illustrated artist, I will create and design t-shirts and other items per a client's request and use embroidery to print logos on baseball caps and casual wear.

Finally, I am learning how to drive. I have put it off long enough!

To all who have endured struggles—I believe that you are capable of doing anything. No one, including yourself, should say that you aren't capable. There are others who are willing to help you overcome this struggle. Once you're either educated by them, or yourself, invest into your talent(s) everyday so you'll be able to recall your knowledge of those talents easily.

I've achieved my goal, and this would be a good time to bring my book to a close. It's the evening of my 26th birthday, August 25, 2020. My mom and I celebrated at Board and Brush Creative Studio in Port St. Lucie, Florida with Olivia Anna Giamanco. Olivia encouraged me three years ago to continue the dream of writing my autobiography. She has been an inspiration to me over the years and I could not think of a better person to have celebrated this special milestone with. I will always be grateful for all that she has done. May God bless you Olivia, for your kind and caring spirit for individuals diagnosed with Autism Spectrum Disorder.

To the individuals who have crossed my path during this amazing journey, especially my Christ Fellowship Church family and leadership teams, I just want to say thank you to each one of you. To my siblings, my Dad, and most of all my Mom… you are the wind beneath my wings and the journey is not over, it's just beginning.

"The End"

Olivia, Mom and I at Board and Brush Creative Studio in Port St. Lucie for my 26th birthday.

The sky is the limit!!
There is a whole new world out there waiting for me to discover.

The only cookbooks I enjoy using when I am in the kitchen, Magnolia Table Volumes 1 and 2.

"My Favorites List"
Barack Obama
Michelle Obama
Oprah Winfrey
Tyler Perry
Shelton Jackson Lee, aka Spike Lee
Jimmy Fallon
Stephen Spielberg
Walt Disney
Dan Akroyd
Iris Apfel-Business Woman, Interior Designer and Fashion Icon
John C. Maxwell-Author, Speaker, Pastor
Christ Fellowship, Palm Beach Garden, Florida
Face the Nation
CBS Sunday Morning
Meet the Press
Good Morning America
ABC World News Tonight with David Muir
Ellen DeGeneres- Ellen DeGeneres Show
Portia de Rossi- The Ellen Fund
The View
The Talk
Tamron Hall
Kelly Clarkson
Last Man Standing- Actress Amanda Fuller
Chip and Joanna Gaines Magnolia Table/Magnolia Network
Apple, Inc.
Bill Nye the Science Guy
The Magic School Bus
Star Wars Trilogies
Captain America
Marvel Adventures
Chadwick Boseman
Joe and Anthony Russo

Holly Robinson Peete and cast- For Peete's Sake
Rodney Peete Jr. (R.J.)-
For Peete's Sake
Steve Harvey-Family Feud and Celebrity Family Feud
Jack Nicklaus
Ben Carson- Gifted Hands
Tony Awards
Oscar Awards
Emmy Awards
Grammy Awards
America's Got Talent
America's Funniest Home Video

The individuals that I have included on my favorite list have had a huge impact on my life and through their accomplishments it has encouraged me to pursue my "DREAMS"

-William Rose-

This is a photo of my Christ Fellowship Leadership Team. They have continued to be there to support me whenever I call on them.

Photo Gallery

Great family friends, Marie-Helene Clarck, Nolwenn Clarck, and Mom

My sister Meridith and I taking a photo together, prior to me leaving to enjoy my Prom night.

Mom, Meridith, and I at Christ Fellowship during the Christmas Holidays.

Caleb Castille an Actor in Woodlawn (2015) and former cornerback for the Crimson Tide at the University of Alabama took a few photos with me at my home church, Christ Fellowship in Palm Beach Gardens, Florida.

Enjoying a day at the Grand Canyon.

Las Vegas, a trip I will never forget.

My trip to California was spectacular. Dana Point was my favorite spot.

I will always cherish the memories I have of my visit to the Twin Towers Memorial in New York.

Time Square in New York, there is no place like the Big Apple.

My visit to NASA with classmates from Palm Beach State College.

We enjoy giving to the St Lucie County Sheriff Office.
Mom and I presenting donated baked goods to Sheriff Ken Mascara.

Illustrated Art

A self-portrait I drew of myself in middle school at the age of 13.

Illustrated Art

An image I drew of one of my characters during high school in 2012.

Illustrated Art

Characters I drew after I regained my skills in 2016.
I lost my ability to draw after the stress I unfortunately endured at the university I attended after high school.

Graphic Design Art

Graphic Design Art

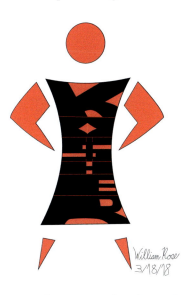

Kosher Apparel was a graphic design I created while at Palm Beach State College in 2018.

This animal totem project of a father and son was designed at Palm Beach State College in 2018.

Illustrated Art

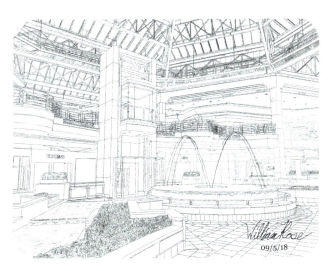

This high-detailed sketch of the Gardens Mall was created in 2018.

Graphic Design Art   Illustrated Art

This Rose Magazine cover design was created for   Walt Disney illustrated drawing at
a project at Palm Beach State College in 2019.   Jupiter High School in 2013.

Illustrated Art

A Metropolitan Museum of Art book scale illustration I drew at Palm Beach State College in 2019.

Graphic Design Art

A logo I designed for Women United for Autism, LLC in 2020.

Resources

Women United for Autism, L.L.C.
womenunitedforautism.com
womenunitedforautism@gmail.com
info@womenunitedforautism.com
Terri Rose Employment Network
Terriroseenetwork.com
terriroseemploymentnetwork@gmail.com
info@terriroseemploymentnetwork.com
Social Security Administration
ssa.gov
National Institutes of Health
nih.gov
The National Institute of Mental Health
Nimh.nih.gov
Palm Beach State College (PBSC)
Center for Student Accessibility
(CSA)
palmbeachstate.edu
Palm Beach School for Autism
pbsfa.org
JARC Florida (Jewish Association for Residential Care)
jarcfl.org
Haley Moss
haleymoss.net
IDEA
https://sites.ed.gov/idea/

South Florida Society for Arts and Culture
http://www.southfloridafinearts.org
Palm Beach Children's Chorus, Inc.
pbchildrenschorus.org
Virtual Children's Chorus
virtualchildrenschorus.com
Florida Atlantic University (FAU)
Student Accessibility Services
fau.edu
Office for Civil Rights
hhs.gov/ocr
Agency for Persons with Disabilities
apdcares.org
Disability Rights Florida
disabilityrightsflorida.org
Family Network on Disabilities
fndusa.org
Coalition for Independent Living Options
cilo.org
Florida Atlantic University CARD
(Center for Autism and Related Disabilities)
autism.fau.edu
The Dan Marino Foundation
danmarinofoundation.org
University of Miami-Nova Southeastern University CARD (Center for Autism and Related Disabilities)
umcard.org
Palm Beach Habilitation Center
pbhab.com
El's for Autism Foundation
elsforautism.org
The Chocolate Spectrum
thechocolatespectrum.org
Palm Beach County Education Opportunities Children with Special Needs
www.pbcedu.org/students-with-special-needs/

Martin County School District
Exceptional Student Education
martinschools.org
Deliver the Dream
deliverthedream.org
Special Olympics Florida
specialolympicsflorida.org
Florida Atlantic University (FAU)
Academy for Community Inclusion (ACI)
https://www.fau.edu/education/academicdepartments/ese/aci/
Toast Masters International
https://www.toastmasters.org

Photo and Illustration Credits

Grad Images
Prestige Portraits
William Andrew Rose
Cathy Feld
Joan Therien
Dorothy A. Shaw

Acknowledgements

Meridith Rose
Andrea Macon
Michelle Poitevint
Bettye W. Knighton
Carolyn Moses

Endorsement

William Rose personifies Amazing Grace, Amazing Gifts. He is a gifted artist. I am so impressed by the amazing talent and work ethic that William possesses. His story is truly one of amazing grace. Being in the presence of this exceptional young man inspired me to reach for higher heights and effectively use all the gifts I've been given. William has a story to tell. I promise you will be moved by the story of this amazing young man. I wholeheartedly endorse William's book, Amazing Grace, Amazing Gifts. It will leave you with a deep appreciation for the hope that young men such as William offer the world.

Dr. Bettye W. Knighton, CEO
Majestically Speaking
www.speakbettye.com

Mom; Terri Cunningham Rose, Dad; Keith Rose and I after the Academic Excellence and Leadership Awards Ceremony at the Wyndham Grand Jupiter, Florida

About the Author, William Andrew Rose

As an individual diagnosed with high functioning autism, William Rose has faced many challenges, especially in the areas of communication and executive functioning. Despite the impact that it has had on his ability to effectively communicate with others, through his faith he has persevered. He is a brother to three siblings, musician, writer, illustrated artist with an Associate of Science degree in Graphic Design Technology, member of Toast Masters International, photographer and serves on the Leadership Team at his home church Christ Fellowship, Palm Beach Gardens, Florida. William enjoys cooking, reading, gaming, bike riding, golfing, and traveling. Connect with him at info@williamandrewroseproductions.com

About the Author, Terri Cunningham Rose

Terri Cunningham Rose is an entrepreneur and the owner of three organizations: Women United for Autism, L.L.C., Empower Employ You, Inc., and TREN-Terri Rose Employment Network. She is also the founder and executive director of H.A.L.E.E. Inc., a 501c-3 non-profit organization that she established in 2000. Her agency provides employment services for disabled children, adults, and Ticket to Work holders. Terri holds a Bachelor of Science degree in Organizational Management. She is the mother of four adult children, speaker, life coach, educator, writer, blogger, advocate, and community leader. Terri enjoys cooking, gardening, sewing, reading, traveling and donating her time to assist mothers of children diagnosed with autism spectrum disorder. Connect with her at info@womenunitedforautism.com or www.womenunitedforautism.com